CURIOUS PET

MY FRIEND THE IGUANA

JOANNE RANDOLPH

WINDMILL BOOKS
New York

Published in 2011 by Windmill Books, LLC
303 Park Avenue South, Suite # 1280, New York, NY 10010-3657

First Edition

Editor: Jennifer Way
Book Design: Erica Clendening
Layout Design: Julio Gil
Photo Researcher: Brian Garvey

Photo Credits: Cover, pp. 5, 7, 8, 11, 12, 13, 17, 21 Shutterstock.com; p. 4 AFP/Getty Images; p. 6 Tim Flach/Getty Images; p. 9 © Biosphoto/Sylvain Cordier/Peter Arnold Inc.; p. 10 SW Productions/Getty Images; p. 14 © Juniors Bildarchiv/age fotostock; p. 15 Reinhard Dirscherl/Visuals Unlimited, Inc./Getty Images; p. 16 © Jordi Cami/age fotostock; p. 18 © www.iStockphoto/Wojciech Wojcik; p. 19 © www.iStockphoto/Susan Reid; p. 20 Wendy Ashton/Getty Images.

Library of Congress Cataloging-in-Publication Data

Randolph, Joanne.
My friend the iguana / by Joanne Randolph.
p. cm. — (Curious pet pals)
Includes index.
ISBN 978-1-60754-977-2 (library binding) — ISBN 978-1-60754-985-7 (pbk.) — ISBN 978-1-60754-986-4 (6-pack)
1. Iguanas as pets—Juvenile literature. I. Title.
SF459.I38R36 2011
639.3'95—dc22
2010004697

Manufactured in the United States of America

For more great fiction and nonfiction, go to www.windmillbooks.com

CPSIA Compliance Information: Batch # BW2011WM: For Further Information contact Windmill Books, New York, New York at 1-866-478-0556

Contents

MEET THE IGUANA

When you think of a pet you might think of a dog or a cat. But have you ever thought about having a pet that has **scales**?

Iguanas are lizards. Iguanas are covered in scales, as snakes are.

Reptiles can make great pets. Snakes, turtles, and lizards are all reptiles.

Iguanas like to climb. You should put branches or shelves in their cage for them to climb.

Iguanas are one kind of lizard that people keep as pets. There are many different kinds of iguanas. The most common kind kept as a pet is the green iguana.

Is an iguana the right pet for you? You need to find out as much about these lizards as you can.

Most iguanas have good eyesight. They use their eyesight to catch food and avoid predators.

It is important to find out what iguanas need to be healthy and happy pets. It also is important to understand their behavior, or how they act.

Iguanas are active, curious, and smart. They are quiet, too. Iguanas like to climb and some even like to swim. They are fun friends to watch!

Owning an iguana is not the same as owning a dog or cat. Unlike dogs and cats, iguanas are not cuddly animals.

Iguanas can be many different colors. The one shown here has patches of bright red and orange.

It might take a while before your iguana is comfortable being held by you.

Iguanas like to lie on a sunny rock in the wild to warm up. In your house, a warm spot by the window might be a good place for your iguana.

Iguanas are reptiles. Reptiles are **cold-blooded**. This means that iguanas cannot warm or cool their own bodies. In the wild they would count on sunlight to warm them. In your home, they will need special lamps where they can sun themselves.

Iguanas are not naturally social animals. This means that they don't always like being around other animals and people the way that dogs and cats do.

These kids are enjoying watching a young pet iguana.

Iguanas like quiet. They like to be alone. This does not mean that your iguana will not enjoy being with you. It just takes time.

It will take time for you to build a relationship with your iguana. Don't try to hold it or touch it right away. The iguana wants to be sure that you are not planning to hurt it or to eat it. Loud noises and quick movements make iguanas worry.

Iguana Needs and Care

Baby iguanas are about 6 inches (15 cm) long. Full-grown iguanas can be up to 6 feet (2 m) long from head to tail. They can weigh up to 30 pounds (14 kg).

This young iguana is shedding its skin.

Iguanas need lots of space to be happy. A 4-foot (1.2 m) iguana needs a cage that is 6 feet long (1.8) by 6 feet (1.8 m) high.

A baby iguana can fit on one hand.

Iguanas need branches to climb and leaves to hide in. They need water for drinking, bathing, and swimming.

It is important to learn about what your pet iguana needs to stay healthy and happy. An iguana's cage needs to

You can use a wire or a glass cage for your iguana. Wire cages can give pet lizards like this one more fresh air.

be lined on the bottom with wood chips, gravel, or newspapers. This lining needs to be changed often. Iguanas also need healthy foods and clean water.

In the wild, iguanas can use the water as a way to get away from enemies. Some love to swim, while others would rather stay up in the trees.

Iguanas also need to be bathed at least once a week. If you put a tub or large bowl of water in your iguana's living space, it will bathe itself!

In the wild, iguanas grow long, sharp **claws.** They use these claws to climb. They use them to **defend** themselves against enemies, too.

It is important to take your iguana to the vet for regular checkups. Be sure to pick a vet who is familiar with reptiles.

Hopefully, your pet iguana will learn that you are a friend. Even so, you will need to trim, or cut, your iguana's

Iguanas claws grow long and sharp.

claws so that you won't get scratched. The claws need to be trimmed every few weeks. You can ask your **vet** to show you how to do this safely.

IGUANA DIET

The best way to keep your pet iguana healthy is to make sure you feed it healthy foods. Iguanas are mainly herbivores.

This iguana is eating a banana. Iguanas should be offered a lot of choices. Eating the same thing every day can get boring for them, just as it can for you.

This means they eat mostly plants. They need to eat lots of different vegetables, leafy greens, and some fruits.

Iguanas should be fed lots of dark greens, but not iceberg lettuce. Hand feeding your iguana helps it to trust you.

You can buy special iguana food at the pet store. However, your pet iguana should still get fresh food as well. Feeding iguanas different kinds of food keeps them happy as well as healthy.

Every pet is different. Some iguanas get used to being held. They may even sit on their owners' shoulders. Other iguanas may never do this.

Iguanas can be friendly family pets. They may like to be with you and sit on your shoulder.

One of the most important parts of having a pet is learning to respect it.

Every kind of iguana is having trouble in the wild. Today there are many iguana farms. This means wild iguanas can be left alone and people can still enjoy these interesting pets!

Do not try to make it do something it does not want to do. Over time, you may find your pet lets you hold it more. Either way, it will be a fun, one-of-a-kind pet!

GUESS WHAT?

There are 700 kinds of iguanas, including desert iguanas, rock iguanas, and chuckwallas.

The biggest iguana is the rock iguana, which is sometimes called the rhinoceros iguana.

An iguana's tail can break off. If an enemy catches hold of the tail, it breaks free from the iguana's body. The tail will usually grow back.

An iguana needs around 6 to 8 hours of sunlight or light from a special lamp each day.

An iguana likes its home to be 85–90° F (29–32° C) during the day. It can be a bit cooler at night. It also needs to be humid, or wet.

GLOSSARY

CLAWS (KLAWZ) The sharp parts of an animal's feet.

COLD-BLOODED (KOHLD-bluh-did) Having body heat that changes with the heat around the body.

DEFEND (dih-FEND) To guard from harm.

REPTILES (REP-tylz) Cold-blooded animals with thin, dry pieces of skin called scales.

RESPECT (rih-SPEKT) To think highly of someone or something.

SCALES (SKAYLZ) The thin, dry pieces of skin that form the outer covering of snakes, lizards, and other reptiles.

VET (VET) A doctor who treats animals.

READ MORE

Rosenthal, Karen, DVM. *The Iguana: An Owner's Guide to a Happy Healthy Pet*. New York: Howell Book House, 2001.

Simon, Elizabeth. *Iguana*. New York: Weigl Publishers, 2005.

Williams, Sara. *101 Facts About Iguanas*. Milwaukee, Wisconsin: Gareth Stevens Publishers, 2001.

INDEX

WEB SITES

For Web resources related to the subject of this book, go to: www.windmillbooks.com/weblinks and select this book's title.